31

Word Decrees
That Will
Revolutionize
Your Life

31 Word Decrees That Will Revolutionize Your Life
Written by Kevin and Kathy Basconi exclusively for:
King of Glory Ministries International Publications 2011

ISBN 978-0-9833152-0-9
This printing 2015.

King of Glory Ministries International,
P O Box 903,
Moravian Falls, NC 28654
 336-818-1210 or 828-320-3502
www.kingofgloryministries.org

Cover Design and layout by Kevin Basconi
Printed in the United States of America

*Unless otherwise indicated, all scripture quotations are taken
from the New King James Version of the Bible.*

Dedication

This

book

Is

dedicated

to

God the Father, God the Son, and God the Holy Spirit

without

You

Guys

none

of

this

would

have

been

possible!

Kevin's heart to see the Body of Christ changed and transformed amazes me. This book positions you for breakthrough in your life and renews your mind by transforming the way you think. Every day is a new day we get to experience the goodness of God and His plans and purposes for us. There is something from God's word for you each day preparing your heart and thinking processes so the will of God may best be displayed in your life.

Robert Ward, Redding, CA

Contents

Introduction

The Bible tells us that the Word of God is sharp and alive! *"For the word of God is living and powerful, and sharper than any two-edged sword, piercing even to the division of soul and spirit, and of joints and marrow, and is a discerner of the thoughts and intents of the heart"* (Hebrews 4:12). God's anointed Word is life changing.

As a new believer in this Man named Jesus Christ, I began to develop a supernatural hunger for God's Word. There was just "something" deep down within me that needed to be fed the scriptures. I now know that this was the "real me," my spirit, that had been starving for the Bread of Life for over forty years! We need to feed our spirits and souls everyday just like we feed our bodies food.

Jesus encouraged us, *"Man shall not live by bread alone, but by every word of God"* (Luke 4:4). As a new Christian I discovered that when I read and spoke God's word over my life my days were much more peaceful and I did not struggle.

You see, from the moment that I prayed to receive Jesus Christ as my Lord and Savior, I was instantly set free from a thirty year lifestyle of drug and alcohol addiction. (Kevin shares this testimony in great detail on his CD *From the Gutter to Glory,* available for FREE in the ministry Resource Center on our web page).

One day while I was working I was listening to the radio, and I heard a man speaking about 1 Chronicles 4:10. This passage of scripture is commonly known as the prayer of Jabez.

So I began to pray that prayer over my life every day. I would pray the prayer of Jabez numerous times and I would speak it out audibly as I went about my daily business.

"Oh, that You would bless me indeed, and enlarge my territory, that Your hand would be with me, and that You would keep me from evil, that I may not cause pain!" So God granted him what he requested.

I would tailor the prayer of Jabez to my immediate needs. For example, if my rent was due I would pray something like this:

Lord, I thank You that You are going to bless me indeed. Lord, bless me in a great and mighty way. Lord, I thank You that You are going to put Your hands upon me and bless me and expand my territory in my finances so that I can pay my rent. And, Lord, I thank You that You're going to keep me from evil that it is not going to cause any pain. Amen.

Incidentally, I was never late nor missed any of my rent payments during this period of strife. I was learning to depend upon God. This was despite the fact that I was poverty stricken. In the natural way of looking at my situation, there often seemed to be no way to make my rent. But God was always faithful to supernaturally supply my needs in this season!

Hallelujah! Glory to God in the highest! Jesus Christ of Nazareth still reigns upon the earth today!

Momma Dowell

To my amazement, I soon discovered that these prayers, along with God's word, rapidly changed my circumstances. This transformation came supernaturally fast as I decreed them over my life. During this time the Lord sent a wonderful Spirit-filled mentor into my life. Her name was Omega Dowell. Momma Dowell taught me a lot more about the importance of speaking God's word out loud over my life. She always told everyone, "I am truly blessed and highly favored with Divine intervention in my life today, and I am walking in the FOG, the favor of God."

So I added this positive word confession to my daily custom of decreeing, speaking, and praying God's word. I spoke positive statements over my life and circumstances each and every day. You see, I was poor. I was sick. I was in debt. I was coming out of a very dark place of addictions, hopelessness, and rejection.

But I saw that the Bible said that I was to prosper and be in health (3 John 1:2). I saw where the scriptures said that I was God's child through my simple faith in Jesus Christ (Romans 8:14; Galatians 3:26). The word of God taught me that I was healed (Matthew 8:17; I Peter 2:24; Isaiah 53:4).

After a while, I started to wonder why I was oppressed with poverty and sickness. If the Bible was real, if the word of God was really true, I should not be struggling with hopelessness, sickness, poverty, and rejection. But I was. That was a fact. I started to ask God about this.

Praise God! The precious Holy Spirit began to speak gently to me. You know that the Holy Spirit will speak to you as a man does to a friend. He said: "*Put Me in remembrance of My promises to you.*" (See Isaiah 43:26.) At the time I did not know that this phrase was actually in the Bible. However, I redoubled my efforts and began to remind God of what the Bible said about me. I persistently reminded the Lord.

I continued to decree and to speak God's scriptures and Momma Dowell's word confession over my life all the time. I prayed the prayer of Jabez nearly continuously. Even to this day, when I pray for my enemies I pray the prayer of Jabez for them (Matthew 5:44).

At night, I would recline upon my bed and remind Jesus what His word promised me before I went to sleep. And then I would thank Him that I was prosperous and blessed. I would thank Him that I was healed, even though, in the natural realm, I was poor, sick, and my life was quite problematic and tough.

I just thanked Him and went to sleep with a smile on my face! I just praised God because He was going to prosper me. I just thanked the Lord that He was going to heal me. I did this every day for about three months. During this time I also studied and read God's Word constantly. Actually, although my life was still a mess in the natural, this was a wonderful season of drawing near to the Lord.

I was feeding my spirit with the Bread of Life just like Jesus had encouraged us to do. Something else rather remarkable and quite supernatural began to happen. As I searched for God in His word, the God of the Bible began to draw close to me. James 4:8 promises us this: *"Draw near to God and He will draw near to you."*

It was during this season that I first began to have angelic encounters. These supernatural experiences served to transform my mindset about the reality of God's Kingdom.

(You can learn more about these angelic visitations and more truth about God's angels in Kevin's trilogy of books titled *The Reality of Angelic Ministry Today*. These books, and many CD and Mp3 teachings on the subject of angelic ministry are available in our on-line Book Store. www.kingofgloryministries.org/store.)

That is one of the wonderful and supernatural benefits of decreeing God's anointed word over your life. You will draw closer to Jesus and He will draw closer to you. That is really what this life is all about. We need more of the Messiah, and I pray that this book will help you to walk closer to Him than ever before. Jesus wants to walk very near to you everywhere you go each day.

On November 25, 2001, I had a visitation of the Lord Jesus, and I experienced His supernatural love. I cannot express in the English language the magnitude of the Love that the Savior of the world has for you.

The Son of God is yearning to be in intimate fellowship with you and His love for you is more extravagant and mind-blowing than you could ever imagine. Someone should write a song about that; *I can only imagine* what it might sound like.

Nuts!

People, mostly Christian people, began to wonder if I may have been losing my mind. I mean a lot of people felt sorry for me. I was poor. I was sick. I had lost almost everything that I had ever owned.

But when they would see me in the store or bump into me in the street or in the church and ask me how I was doing, I would always tell them this, "I am truly blessed and highly favored, with great grace, and Divine intervention in my life today. I am a King's kid. I am a royal priest after the order of Melchizedek, and I am walking in the FOG, the favor of God!" I can still remember the look of pity that some of them tried to hide on their faces.

They sought to conceal their feelings with a false smile. "That is nice," they would say, even though they didn't believe a word of it. Most folks would just scamper away a little too quickly giving me a perplexed glance over their shoulders.

They thought I was nuts! I was living in poverty, but I kept telling them that I was truly blessed! I was living in a tiny house in a crack neighborhood, but I kept telling them that I was highly favored! Most people were aware that I was living on ramen noodles and Kool-Aid, but I was declaring that I was a King's kid! Nuts, they thought!

As a matter of fact, I learned later that many people (in and out of the church) were taking bets on how long I would stay sober and walk with Jesus. Well, as of this writing, it's been a decade and I'm still going stronger than ever by the grace of God! Hallelujah! He is good!

It did not take long before people realized that when they asked me off-handedly how I was doing I would recite Momma Dowell's word decree to them. So, several people stopped asking me, "How are you doing today?"

Usually we really don't care, do we? It is just something that we say by habit. We don't really care or actually want to know at times, do we? But I looked for every opportunity to speak Momma Dowell's decrees out over my life.

I still do today. Anytime a clerk at a checkout counter asks me how I am doing, I let her rip, "I am truly blessed and highly favored, with great great grace and Divine intervention in my life today. I am a King's kid. I am a royal priest after the order of Melchizedek, and I am walking in the FOG!"

Then they usually look at me like a deer in the headlights with their mouths hanging open. They stare at me frozen by the power of my words for a moment as if locked in unbelief!

So I preach to them. I say: "Do you want to know what the FOG is?" That usually jars them back to movement, and they often flutter their eyelids and continue to stare at me blankly. Not everyone wants to know what the FOG is.

One time someone thought that I was talking about some kind of new designer drug.

They thought that I was high, or under the influence of FOG. I was. I was as high as a kite on the Most High God! But I go ahead and tell them all about the FOG anyway; "It is the favor of God! How are you doing today?"

They give me an opportunity to speak my prophetic decree over my life based upon God's anointed word! So I go for it! You should go for it too. Sure, at times these folks may think that you are nuts, but that's ok! By the way, you can feel free to appropriate my word decrees and speak them liberally over your life too.

God's word is freely available to anyone who wishes to make good use of it to help change their lives.

I am sure if you do that, Momma Dowell will be smiling down at you from the great cloud of witnesses. She would probably say, "Hallelujah, that one is truly blessed and highly favored now!"

Stand Firm

There is an old axiom that says: "If you don't stand for something, you will fall for anything."

I like to make a stand for Jesus. Anytime, or anywhere, I love to declare His Holy name, the name that is above every other name, the name that every creature in heaven and earth will bow their knees to.

Yes, I praise His Holy name! I want to stand on that name. I want to stand firm on the Cornerstone, and Rock of my salvation! Hallelujah! My friend, where do you stand today?

When we speak the name of Jesus, there is power in that name. The Lord gave us the right to use His name, and it still carries the same power and authority that it did when Jesus walked upon the earth.

You know the disciples never prayed in the name of Jesus while they walked with Him. It was only after Jesus Christ was crucified to make atonement for mankind that we were given the right to speak and to pray in His name. Only after the Messiah shed His precious blood to make payment in full for the cleansing of our sins were we given the right to pray and to speak the name of Jesus over our life and circumstances.

It was only after Jesus died upon the Cross of Calvary and was buried in that unused grave. It was only after the Lord was raised from the dead that He empowered you and me to use His Holy name.

Praise God, we do have the privilege and authority to pray and speak in the name of Jesus Christ of Nazareth today. Why? So that our joy may be full, complete, lacking no worthy or good thing, that is why. The name of Jesus carries in it prosperity, favor, healing, and total salvation for our spirit, soul, and body.

Jesus makes this powerful promise in John 16: 23-24:

And in that day you will ask Me nothing. Most assuredly, I say to you, whatever you ask the Father in My name He will give you. Until now you have asked nothing in My name. Ask, and you will receive, that your joy may be full.

Jesus prophesied that the day would come when we would not ask Him for anything. Why? because Jesus understood that He was to be crucified, buried, and that on the third day He would rise from the dead.

To God be the glory! He did. And when Jesus rose from the dead (past tense), He ascended upon High to sit on His throne as the King of kings and the Lord of lords.

Jesus blazed a trail into the heavens to the very presence and right hand of the Father. And we can freely follow Him, because He was our Forerunner. Look at what Hebrews 6:20 tells us:

Where the forerunner has entered for us, even Jesus, having become High Priest forever according to the order of Melchizedek.

Jesus set the example for you and me. We are to be kings and priests before God the Father.

That is how we can actually come boldly before God's throne of power to obtain mercy and grace in our times of need (Hebrews 4:16).

Ephesians 4:8 also clearly illustrates this aspect of Christ's Passion:

Therefore He says: "When He ascended on high, He led captivity captive, and gave gifts to men.

What was one of the primary gifts that He gave to men? His name. Jesus gave us the power to pray to the Father in His name.

He prophesied that in "that day" we would not pray to Him or need to ask Him anything. He said that His followers had not asked or prayed in His name up to then (before He was crucified).

I encourage you to take some time and to search the gospels of Matthew, Luke, Mark, and John. You will find that this is really true. They did not pray in the name of Jesus in the three years that they walked with the Messiah.

Jesus told us that when "that day" came we would have the liberty, right, authority, and privilege to ask the Father for whatever in the name of Jesus Christ and that God the Father *will* give you whatever you ask Him for. Whatever means anything! Of course we need to ask according to His will.

What was "that day?" It was the day He suffered on Calvary and then ascended to the Right Hand of the Father. We are living in that day! Hallelujah!

What a time to be alive! The God who created the heavens and the earth with His Words has given you and me the right and authority to ask Him for anything in the mighty name of Jesus Christ of Nazareth, and He has promised to do whatever we ask!

Learn to use that name. Learn to stand upon that name. Learn who you are in the name of Christ! You are a king and priest who has been cleansed by the blood of Christ to minister to our God and Father.

At the moment I was delivered from drugs, I was translated into Christ's Kingdom of Light instantly!

I was transformed into a king and a priest instantly. I was plucked from the kingdom of darkness and transferred instantly into the Kingdom of God's Holy Light. I was engrafted into the Lord's family. I became a joint heir with Christ and was freely given an eternal inheritance that was laid up for me in heaven. If you want to be born again, or saved, you will also be transferred instantly into the Kingdom of God's Holy Light. You will also reap all of those same rewards and supernatural blessings!

Hallelujah!

Kings and Priests

Revelation 5:10 also encourages us that Christ's Blood has transformed us and made us "*kings and priests to our God; And we shall reign on the earth.*"

Did you catch that last part? We are to reign on earth. This is not talking about in the great bye and bye, when our bodies die and we go on to heaven in the form of our regenerated spirit man. No, this is speaking about ruling and reigning in this life, right now, today!

How? Through the limitless power that has been given to you and me to commission and employ the very name of the Son of God, Jesus Christ of Nazareth, to work on our behalf!

There is power in the name of Jesus. Begin to learn how to wield it as a mighty weapon. Decree and call those things that do not exist into existence as you confess God's anointed word in the name of Jesus Christ of Nazareth!

The truth is that you will possess the things that you confess!

The name of Jesus Christ is a wonderful and blessed spiritual gift that you can employ as you speak God's word found in the 31 short decrees in this book. There is power, wonder working power, in the name of the Lamb!

Learn to use the name of Jesus Christ as you work, pray, and go about your day! It works! So purpose in your heart to confess, decree, and speak God's promises over your life every day!

Stand firm as a royal king and priest (or queen and priestess) on the anointed word of God in the mighty and magnificent name of Jesus Christ of Nazareth!

When you begin to speak the name of Jesus Christ over your life and circumstances, things begin to change. Every demon in hell must bow to that Name. And every angel in heaven will heed Gods anointed word spoken in the name of Jesus Christ of Nazareth (Psalm 103:20).

So as you begin to speak and decree the confessions of God's anointed word in this book, expect your life to be transformed by the power of the name of Jesus Christ of Nazareth!

A Transformed Life
Walking in the FOG!

You know what? It did not take God long to begin to honor my confessions of faith. In less than two years, the Lord transformed my life. Jesus took me from sickness to health. The Lord supernaturally took me from poverty to prosperity, from the gutter to glory, and launched me into international ministry almost overnight! Glory to God!

How? I began to confess, decree, and speak His word over my life and circumstances. I began to put the power in the name of Jesus Christ to work on my behalf, and you can too.

He totally transformed my life and today the **fact is** that **I am** truly blessed and highly favored, with great, great grace, and Divine intervention in my life. I am a King's kid. I am a royal priest after the order of Melchizedek, and *I am walking in the FOG! Whoo-weee!*

God transformed my life when I acted upon the Spirit's gentle prompting to put Him in remembrance of His promises to me. Years later, I discovered this scripture and began to have a Hallelujah fit!

Isaiah 43:26:

Put Me in remembrance; Let us contend together; State your case, that you may be acquitted.

You see sometimes our spirits know a whole lot more than our unregenerate minds and souls do. God speaks to His children Spirit to spirit. We need to learn to pay attention to our recreated spirits more! The Holy Spirit spoke to my spirit using a scripture from the Old Testament.

So, as you confess the decrees of God's word found in this little book every day, you will be putting the Father in remembrance of His promises to you. His word promises that He *will* contend together with you for your breakthrough, or acquittal.

The God of the universe will help you fight your battle, and if God be for us who can stand against us (Romans 8:31)?

Learn to Recognize the Voice of God

I was not familiar with the scripture that was spoken to me, but I *was* learning to recognize the voice of the Holy Spirit. This was a learning curve. It was a process as I began to hear the voice of God clearly, but He was speaking to me. He is most likely speaking to you too.

It may also be a learning curve and a process with you as you learn to recognize the voice of God. However, if you are diligent to listen, He will begin to speak to you in a very clear and recognizable way.

Scripture encourages us that we are God's people, and that we are the people of His pasture. We are the sheep of His hand. That is a comforting thought, isn't it? As His sheep we can hear His voice, because the Lord desires to have fellowship and intimacy with us. He loves us and wants to talk to us about every aspect of our lives and walk with Him (Psalm 95:7-8).

Remember the words of the Messiah:

My sheep hear My voice, and I know them, and they follow Me. And I give them eternal life, and they shall never perish; neither shall anyone snatch them out of My hand (John 10:27-28).

So I want to encourage you that you can hear the Lord as He speaks to you in your daily life and activities.

Today as a believer in Jesus you have the Holy Spirit which dwells inside of you (1 Corinthians 3:16).

There are times that the Holy Spirit speaks very clearly. He was sent from on high to guide and teach us. If we will open our hearts, He will speak to us as a friend and help us in every aspect of our lives. The Holy Spirit spoke clearly in Acts 13:2: "*The **Holy Spirit said**, 'Now separate to Me Barnabas and Saul for the work'*" *(emphasis added).*

The precious Holy Spirit is still speaking today, and if we position ourselves, it is actually easy to hear what He is saying to us. The Holy Spirit will always draw you closer to the Messiah and exalt the Son of God, Jesus Christ.

Jesus told us to expect this ministry of the Holy Spirit saying:

> *"The Helper, the Holy Spirit, whom the Father will send in My name, He will teach you all things, and bring to your remembrance all things that I said to you"* (John 14:26).

In other words the Holy Spirit would teach us, and guide us. The Holy Ghost accomplishes this by speaking to us. He does this in many ways.

But what I want you to understand is that it's important to have your heart open to hear from the Spirit of God. The Holy Ghost was sent to help us in the name of Jesus!

Again, the most common way that God speaks to you is by the Holy Spirit. The indwelling Holy Spirit will speak to you in your spirit, Spirit to spirit. It's important that you learn to hear God's voice.

(For more information about hearing God's voice please read or listen to Kevin Basconi's teaching *"11 Ways That God Is Speaking To You Today"* are available in our on-line Book Store. www.kingofgloryministries.org/store).

Breathed by
the Holy Spirit

In late 2010 and early 2011, the Lord began to speak to me about writing down daily decrees to speak over my life. As I fasted, prayed, and waited upon the Lord, He was faithful to drop the decrees and word confessions that are contained in this little book into my spirit.

He spoke to me Spirit to spirit. Later the Holy Spirit encouraged me to write these word decrees down and to make them available to people so that they could speak them out over their lives too.

Job 22:28 encourages us in this matter: "*You will also declare a thing, And it will be established for you; So light will shine on your ways.*" That is how this little book was birthed.

The book that you're holding in your hands was conceived by the Holy Spirit in a season of prayer and fasting. It was written in less than 96 hours, but it can revolutionize your life! Why? Because the breath of God is upon it! And God's word is *"living and powerful, and sharper than any two-edged sword, piercing even to the division of soul and spirit, and of joints and marrow, and is a discerner of the thoughts and intents of the heart"* (Hebrews 4:12).

I believe with all of my heart that as you decree these short word confessions over your life, you too will see the God of the universe transform your circumstances for the better, just like He did for me.

This is the scriptural principle of Revelation 19:10b: *"The testimony of Jesus **is** the spirit of prophesy!"* (emphasis added).

What the Messiah did for me He can do for you. In fact, Jesus wants to give you a double portion. The Messiah wants to freely give you a greater measure!

Since these word confessions were conceived by the Holy Spirit, I believe that the "Breath of the Spirit" is attached to them. They are alive and active just like Hebrews 4:12 depicts God's Holy word.

God's word can change your life. I have outlined how God's word changed my awful circumstances as I spoke and decreed it over my life and situation. So the breathed word of God can do the same thing for you, because God is no respecter of persons. We are all equal in the eyes of God and He loves us all the same.

What the Lord did for me, He can also do for you. That is the beauty of the Kingdom of Heaven. However, at times it takes some initiative on our part.

Sometimes we have a role to play in releasing the Kingdom of God and the blessings that the Lord has preordained for us to walk in over our lives. Jesus also spoke about this subject too. Praise God! That part is made very easy for us.

We can find out how to activate God's supernatural blessings and favor in our lives by studying the scriptures.

"But Believe"

Sometimes we just need to believe. If we can just muster up the tiniest little bit of faith in God, we can move His hand of blessing and power on our behalf. Jesus will work and move on your behalf because He loves you with an everlasting Love.

It's true. The Father wants to bless you in a great and mighty way. I know it, and you can know it too! So let me encourage you to "but believe" (Jeremiah 31:3).

Mark 11: 22-24 gives us some crystal clear directions along these lines. Jesus said,

> *"Have faith in God. For assuredly, I say to you, whoever **says** [speaks, decrees, confesses, or prophesies] to this mountain, 'Be removed and be cast into the sea,' and does not doubt in his heart, **but believes** that those things he **says** will be done, he will have whatever he **says** [speaks, decrees,*

confesses, or prophesies]." (vv. 22-23, emphasis added).

Do you think that might be important that Jesus instructed us to say (speak, decree, confess, or prophesy) three times? Absolutely, the Lord was aware of the power of our words to create a reality, and to call forth those things that do not exist as if they do (Romans 4:17).

However, verse 24 is the clincher! *"Therefore I say to you, whatever things you ask [speak, decree, confess, or prophesy] when you pray, believe that you receive them, and you will have them."* I just spoke out God's promises to me from my mouth and I purposed in my heart to believe that the Lord's word and promises were true.

It did not matter what it looked like in the natural realm. If the Bible said that I was blessed, healed, and prosperous then I just made a conscious decision to speak that out until my "believer" got that reality absorbed into it.

This is exactly what I would do on my bed ten years ago. I just laid there and reminded Him that His Word said that I was going to proper and be in health (3 John 1:2).

I just put the Lord in remembrance of His Word that Jesus bore all of my sickness on the cross (Matthew 8:17). I actually prophesied to the Lord that I was going to be healed, prospered, and used mightily by Him.

Once I told the Lord that when He gave me a million dollars, I would tithe nine hundred thousand of that money back to His Kingdom. The way that I saw it was that the 10 percent, the one hundred thousand from the one million dollars, would be plenty for me. The Lord was listening! I call this reverse tithing, you should try it!

Did you know that you are supposed to prophesy as you are praying? We are encouraged to challenge God with our prayers (Mark 11:22-24). God dares us to ask Him for something that is too big for Him to do! (Ephesians 3:20). Try to ask God for something too big in prayer, I dare you! Just do it! What do you have to lose?

There is a place in God's Kingdom where we just need to begin to *call forth the invisible realm!* We need to simply speak things into existence!

The Lord has promised to supply all of your needs by His riches in glory by Christ Jesus (Philippians 4:19). You could just as easily say that we can use the name of Jesus to release those promised riches in glory to us as we speak the name of Jesus Christ forth in our prayers.

Sometimes we just need to believe. Really, faith is just acting upon God's written word. As you speak these decrees, you will be acting on God's word and building up your faith!

Confess this out loud right now:

Lord, I choose to believe what Your word says is true. Lord, I thank You that Your word is sharp, alive, and powerful. Lord, I thank You that as I speak Your word over my life, it will go forth and accomplish everything that You said that it would do, and I give You the glory for the good things that are going to come my way as I speak Your word out over my life, In the name of Jesus Christ of Nazareth. Amen! Hallelujah!

Transform Your Life

Now that you have confessed that God's word is active and powerful, you can expect God's anointed word to begin to remove the obstacles and mountains in your life starting immediately. Remember to keep believing and speaking the word over your life and circumstances until the manifestation comes. Don't stop. Just keep acting on what what God's word says.

Romans 4:17-18 also illustrates the Kingdom principle that will make the decrees in this little book work on your behalf:

> *(It is written, "I have made you a father of many nations") in the presence of Him whom he believed—**God, who gives life to the dead and calls those things which do not exist as though they did**; who, contrary to hope, in hope believed, so that he became the father of many nations, according to what was spoken, "So shall your descendants be* (emphasis added).

You can do this—call (speak, decree, confess, or prophesy) those things which do not exist as though they do. It's simple. Speak, or confess Gods anointed word aloud over your life and circumstances, and in hope, simply believe. Don't forget to speak in the name of Jesus Christ of Nazareth.

You'll see God will begin to honor His word and move on your behalf to transform your circumstances and life!

I suggest that you speak all 31 of the decrees in this little book over your life every day for one year.

Perhaps you are a very busy person. Then speak two or three of these word decrees over your life in the morning before you start your day. Speak them out loud and as you begin or end your devotional times in God's word. Speak them out as you make your way to work. Speak them out as you wash the dinner dishes.

Write a few of them on a sticky note and put that on your dashboard. Speak them out as you drive home from work. Decree them as you lie down on your bed to go to sleep.

Put this book in your bathroom and decree them as you use the toilet! Trust me, God does not mind if you talk to Him while you are in the bathroom!

The Holy Ghost talks to me in the shower all the time. I worship Him in there. I pray in the Spirit, and sometimes the glory of God falls. I stand in there weeping in the presence of God and the tangible love of Jesus. I confess these word decrees in there sometimes! You can too.

If you will speak the decrees in this little book in the bathroom, it will give you hundreds of opportunities to confess God's word over your life every month. Remind God of the things that the scriptures promise you in these decrees of His word.

Or, if possible, set aside a little time to speak all 31 decrees out over your life on a daily basis. There is one confession for every day of the month. It won't take too long. This is not hard at all, and it just may revolutionize your life and launch you into your divine destiny.

It really does not matter how you choose to speak these decrees out over your life. Pray and ask the Holy Spirit to guide you in this. He will show you how you should use this little book and its confessions of faith.

One thing that I can promise you is this; it will not take long before the Messiah will attune to your scriptural confessions and decrees of His word (2 Corinthians 9:13; Hebrews 4:14; 10:23).

The Lord will start to contend with you, so that you may be acquitted, prospered, healed, and set free from every yoke and burden of darkness in the mighty name of Jesus Christ of Nazareth!

Now remember that you *ARE* truly blessed and highly favored, with great, great grace, and Divine intervention in your life today. You *ARE* a King's kid. You *ARE* a royal priest after the order of Melchizedek, and **you** can walk in the FOG, the favor of God (Revelation 1:5-6; 5:10).

Jesus said that in Matthew 12:37: *"For by your words you will be justified, and by your words you will be condemned."* The word that was translated "justified", could also be written as "to render or to create." So we can render or create health, favor, prosperity, and grace as we speak those favorable things over our lives in the mighty name of Jesus Christ of Nazareth.

So begin to speak life and not death with your words. So I want to encourage you to guard words. Pray this short prayer;

Lord I ask you to put a guard about my mouth. I choose to speak life and not death with the words of my mouth. Let me say nothing more and nothing less than what you would have me to say today in Jesus name, Amen!

Enforce Your Boundaries

The Bible instructs us to resist the devil (James 4:7). If you have struggled with sickness, poverty, or oppression, you are being harassed by the kingdom of darkness.

However, Jesus has already fought that battle for you and you are more than a conqueror in Christ! The devil is a defeated foe. Jesus already won this war on the cross. So you do not have to fight this battle. The only thing that you are advised to fight in the scriptures is the good fight of faith.

1 Timothy 6:12 makes this point very clear:

> *Fight the good fight of faith, lay hold on eternal life, to which you were also called and have confessed the good confession in the presence of many witnesses.*

You only need to fight the good fight of faith. You don't need to skirmish with the devil. Jesus did that for you already and won that victory by utterly and completely defeating the devil on your behalf. You are encouraged to fight by confessing the good confession of faith in the presence of many witnesses.

In other words, you are taught in the scriptures to fight with the words of your mouth. You are to confess the anointed word of God over your life and circumstances! That is what this little book is designed to help you to do; fight the good fight of faith with confessing or decreeing Gods word audibly with your mouth!

Over time I have discovered that the minions of the evil one are quite naive and most of the time dumb. They do not know that they are defeated, that is why we need to continue to resist the devil by fighting the good fight of faith.

Therefore, you will need to enforce your boundaries and to resist the devil and his minions who are seeking to oppress you.

James 4:7 encourages you: *"Submit to God. Resist the devil and he will flee from you."* The first step is to submit to the Lord Jesus Christ. (If you are not born again or saved, you can pray the prayer of salvation at the end of this book right now and be submitted to God.)

The next step requires you to take action for yourself. You are told to resist the devil. God did not say that He would resist the deceiver for you. Resisting the devil is something that you need to take the initiative and do for yourself.

I cannot do that for you, your husband can't do that for you, your pastor can't do that for you. You have to resist the devil yourself, on your own two feet. You have to stand firm on the Rock of Christ and His word in the Bible.

In other words, we are told that we need to enforce our boundaries. Again, the Lord has given every believer the power and authority to use His mighty name. And we can decree His anointed word and the promises therein over our lives and circumstances every day.

This will establish who we are *"in Christ"* and it is a powerful way to resist the devil.

1 Peter 5:8-10 also gives us keys to enforcing our boundaries:

Be sober, be vigilant; because your adversary the devil walks about like a roaring lion, seeking whom he may devour.

At times the enemy will try to kick you when you are down. That is why we need to resist him by speaking out God's promises of who we are *"in Christ"* every day.

You need to be vigilant, and sober. Don't give any place to the devil. I once heard an old country preacher say, "If you give the devil an inch he will think that he's your ruler." There is a lot of truth in that old saying.

When the enemy hears you speaking out these 31 word confessions, he will realize that you are resisting him and he will have to flee from you. The Bible promises you this, and since it is the word of God it is true!

1 Peter 5:9 continues: *"Resist him* [the devil], *steadfast in the faith."* As you decree Gods word over your life, you are resisting the enemy steadfast in faith. You are standing on the solid Rock of Christ, the anointed word of God, and His covenant promises for your life.

As you declare these scriptural promises, they will begin the process of birthing your divine destiny in the Spirit, and in short order your God-ordained destiny will begin to manifest in the natural realm.

Finally on this point, the Lord has given us a mighty weapon in His word. It is found in Isaiah 54:17. As joint heirs with Christ and sons and daughters of the Most High God, we can appropriate this scripture as our word confession and not only resist the enemy, but soundly defeat him and triumph over him.

> *No weapon formed against you shall prosper, And every tongue which rises against you in judgment You shall condemn. This is the heritage of the servants of the LORD, And their* [your] *righteousness is from Me,"* *Says the LORD.*

You see, sometimes the enemy uses words against us. That is why decreeing God's anointed word over your life is so powerful and life changing. God's word nullifies and triumphs over the enemy's words every time. The enemy's words are the curses that rise against you. These are words inspired of the father of lies.

At times, these word curses can come from well-meaning people, even Christians, doctors, and others that have the right to speak into your life with authority.

Sometimes our own mothers and fathers can unwittingly word curse us with the things that they speak to us. This is especially true for the words spoken to children by a parent.

Have you ever been told that you were "as dumb as an ox" or "clumsy as a mule" by a parent? Then they may have set a word curse in motion over your life. You may need to break the power of those kinds of word curses that have been spoken and decreed over you.

Pray and ask the Holy Spirit to help minister to you in this. He will guide and show you what to do and how to pray to break the power of those kinds of word curses.

Be careful what you hear with your ears. Remember that Jesus even rebuked Peter because of his words in Mark 8:33. Look at how the Messiah enforced His boundaries here:

When He had turned around and looked at His disciples; He rebuked Peter, saying, "Get behind Me, Satan! For you are not mindful of the things of God, but the things of men.

We can also enforce our boundaries like this. Don't be afraid to rebuke someone who is speaking death over your life and circumstances.

I once rebuked my mother's doctor in the name of Jesus Christ of Nazareth. I pointed my right index finger at the red dot on his forehead and said, "I rebuke you in the name of Jesus Christ of Nazareth"!

Incidentally, my mother was healed and did not have any symptoms for about three years after this incident.

Most Christians are bombarded by negative words on a daily basis. Remember that Jesus said that our words were powerful. So at times we need to take a stand and rebuke the words of the enemy no matter who is speaking them over our lives. Of course, we should also practice wisdom and love while doing this.

Look at what the Lord Jesus said in Matthew 12:37: *"For by your words you will be justified, and by your words you will be condemned."*

We need to realize that our words can bring a blessing or a curse (James 3:10-13). At times we can curse ourselves by speaking negative word confessions over our lives.

As a healing minister I have seen literally thousands of people curse themselves, in terms of sickness, with their own words. They may say something like this: "My mother had breast cancer, both of my sisters had breast cancer, and now I have breast cancer. Can you pray for me?"

I can pray for them. However, I always take the time to counsel them to adjust their words and to speak life. By the way we have seen Jesus heal many people of the thing called cancer. To God be the glory!

Instead of saying, "I have cancer," I tell them to say, "I am battling this thing called cancer." I tell them never to say that they "have cancer" because that opens the door for the enemy to put cancer on their bodies. You can have anything that you want or that you say with the words of your mouth.

A Christian can have anything that they want. Anything that you invite to oppress you with the words you speak will gladly attach itself to you. This includes sickness, but that is not God's perfect will for your life. He wants you to prosper and be healthy.

So we need to be very careful in this area. If you say that you have a sickness or weakness, then the devil and his minions will gladly give you a double helping of sickness or weakness.

If you confess poverty, the devil will work double time to keep you poor. If you confess fear, the enemy will work relentlessly to keep you terrified. Resist the devil with your words and the mighty name of Jesus Christ of Nazareth!

So many people give up on life once a doctor decrees death over them with his "prognoses." A doctor may well diagnose you with this or that disease, but you don't have to own it with your words.

Don't go home and tell your loved ones, "I have cancer." No! Realize that you need to begin to enforce your boundaries and speak life over your circumstances.

That is why Isaiah 54:17 is so powerful! It gives you and me the right to condemn "*every tongue which rises against you in judgment.*" You even need to resist the tongue of those in the medical profession, your own family, and friends occasionally.

I am in no way saying that doctors are bad. At times we need them. I go to them myself as the need and occasion arises, but I am careful to listen and do not repeat everything that they diagnose me with. You should be careful "how you hear" too (Luke 8:18).

Why? Because as a child of God your righteousness is from Him. You see, when someone speaks a curse over your life, like cancer, you have the right to command that word curse and the powers of darkness that want to attach to those words to stop in their tracks! Bind them and rebuke them in the name of Jesus Christ of Nazareth.

You have the right to condemn all negative word confessions that are spoken over your life. Enforce your boundaries!

For some of us we need to repent and to renounce the negative words that we have spoken over ourselves and our families with our own tongue. I have heard people say things like "I guess that I will never get out of debt. I will just have to put up with this pain for the rest of my life."

No you don't. You need to repent and get your mind transformed into a Christ-like mind. You need to get into the word of God and begin to confess the word of God that promises to bless you with health and prosperity. You need to repent for speaking a curse over yourself and your family!

Since my daughter was a small child I have always spoken blessings over her life so she could easily hear my words of blessing over her life. I have always told her that she was "a fast runner, talented, the smartest girl in her class, and very beautiful."

Today she is one of the best athletes in her school, she is on the all-state band team (this is only for the most gifted musicians), and she has made straight A's on her last few report cards.

How did that happen? I blessed her with my words and the Lord has brought those things that I have spoken over her to pass. The Lord will do this for you as you speak life and blessings over your children too. By the way, it does not matter how old they are. As grandparents you can still bless your kids with your words!

When I minister in gospel outreach meetings (crusades), in Africa there are usually evil people who want to kill me. I mean literally! There are witch doctors who try to cast demonic spells and incantations upon me.

One time a witch left a dead black mockingbird with its neck broken, hanging in the front of my villa in Tanzania. The message was clear: "We know where you are. We want to kill you and we have placed a curse upon you."

Although I took this threat seriously I was not too concerned. Why? Because the Bible tells me that *He who is in me,* (the Holy Spirit) *is greater than he who is in the world* (1 John 4:4). So Kathy and I just began to decree and confess Isaiah 54:17 over our lives and circumstances.

That prayer and word confession sounded something like this:

> *Right now in the name of Jesus Christ of Nazareth I take authority over every word curse spoken over my life. And I command every evil word, curse, spell, and incantation to fall to the ground right now, in the name of Jesus Christ of Nazareth.*
>
> *I command every demonic power of darkness to loose your assignment against me right now in name of Jesus Christ of Nazareth. I bind you in the name of Jesus Christ of Nazareth, and command you to return to the dry places and to never seek to oppress another person until you are cast into the abyss.*
>
> *Father, I ask you in the mighty name of Jesus Christ of Nazareth to release, loose, and dispatch twelve legions of your angelic host (72,000) to encamp around us and to*

protect us from all plans of the enemy for hurt, harm, or danger, in the name of Jesus Christ of Nazareth. Amen.

This may be an extreme example, but it is a good illustration of this point. Remember that sometimes it can even be our friends and family who unwittingly speak word curses over our lives, so we need to make a practice of enforcing our spiritual boundaries on a daily basis.

On a footnote, we have seen several witch doctors actually accept Jesus Christ as Lord and Savior at our crusade meetings. When they see the power of God present to heal and to work miracles, they get the revelation that Jesus Christ is Lord, and come to the altar to be saved!

So, let's get started decreeing and declaring these 31 life changing confessions now!

I want to really encourage you to persevere. Remember that it took nearly two years for God to totally transform my life. Although, in many ways I started to benefit from the Kingdom of Heaven manifesting in my life right away, and I believe that you will too. Hallelujah!

31

Word Decrees
That Will
Revolutionize
Your Life

Decree 1

I shall serve the Lord with joy and gladness of heart for the abundance of everything that you shall give to me this year. Thank you Lord!

Cornerstone Scripture

2 Corinthians 9:8: *"God is able to make all grace abound toward you, that you, always having all sufficiency in all things, may have an abundance for every good work."*

Decree 2

Thank You, Lord, that I shall be kept in perfect peace and double prosperity as I keep my mind and spirit focused upon You. I choose to trust You today, Father.

Cornerstone Scripture

Isaiah 26:3: *"You will keep him in perfect peace, Whose mind is stayed on You, Because he trusts in You."*

Decree 3

Lord, I will daily cast my cares upon You because You care for me. Right now, Father, I cast these cares upon You. _____.

(Insert concerns or worries of the day in this space.)

Cornerstone Scripture

1 Peter 5:7: *"Cast all your care upon Him, for He cares for you."*

Decree 4

This will be a year of double peace, double grace, and double anointing, and I will prosper and be in health even as my soul prospers. I will prosper in all aspects of my life.

Cornerstone Scripture

3 John 1:2: *"Beloved, I pray that you may prosper in all things and be in health, just as your soul prospers."*

Decree 5

I purpose in my heart and spirit to "let my words be few" in my conversations. I will not enter into vain speaking, evil speaking, or foolish speaking today. Lord, may the meditations of my heart and the words of my mouth be acceptable in Your sight, O LORD, my strength and my redeemer.

Cornerstone Scriptures

Psalm 19:14: *"Let the words of my mouth and the meditation of my heart be acceptable in Your sight, O LORD, my strength and my Redeemer."*

Ecclesiastes 5:2: *"Do not be rash with your mouth, let your words be few."*

Decree 6

The Father's Divine Love, or agape love, has been shed abroad in my heart by the Holy Spirit. I purpose to walk in the God kind of love at all times this day and each day this year. I will love everyone who crosses my path today and I choose to walk in love because the Love of God has been poured out in my heart by the Holy Spirit.

Cornerstone Scripture

Romans 5:5: *"Now hope does not disappoint, because the love of God has been poured out in our hearts by the Holy Spirit who was given to us."*

Decree 7

The Bucket List. Write a list of the ten people who seem to persecute you. Pray for three of them each day until you "pray through" to total forgiveness. Then add the next name on your list to your daily prayer. (Ask the Holy Spirit to help you with this.)

*Prayer: Lord, I purpose in my heart to forgive my enemies and I ask that You would bless _____, _____, and _____ in a great and mighty way this day.

Cornerstone Scripture

Matthew 5:44: *"But I say to you, love your enemies, bless those who curse you, do good to those who hate you, and pray for those who spitefully use you and persecute you."*

Decree 8

Lord, I purpose in my heart to seek first the Kingdom of God and Your righteousness in my life. I will seek Your Kingdom and Your righteousness today and every day. Father, I ask that You will begin to give me more revelation about what Your righteousness encompasses.

Cornerstone Scripture

Matthew 6:33: *"Seek first the kingdom of God and His righteousness, and all these things* [total salvation, prosperity, health, wisdom, love, peace, joy] *shall be added to you."*

Decree 9

I purpose to build myself up by praying in the Spirit today. I will nourish my spirit, soul, and body everyday by praying in the Holy Spirit.

*Now try to pray in the Spirit as long as you can. Pray in the Holy Ghost as you go about your everyday activities today.

*If you are not baptized in the Holy Spirit just pray in your normal fashion.

Cornerstone Scripture

Jude 20: *"But you, beloved, building yourselves up on your most holy faith, praying in the Holy Spirit."*

Decree 10

Lord, I ask You for my inheritance today. Father, I am Your child, and an heir of Your Kingdom. I am a joint-heir with Christ. Father, I thank You for these privileges today. I ask, Lord, for You to release my supernatural heritage as a partaker of the inheritance of the saints of light, because Jesus has delivered me from the power of darkness, and translated me into Your Kingdom of Heaven. Lord, I ask You for the fullness of Christ's Atonement of the Cross of Calvary to come forth in my life and circumstances today. Amen.

Cornerstone Scriptures

Romans 8:17: *"And if children, then heirs—heirs of God and joint heirs with Christ."*

Colossians 1:12-13: *"Give thanks to the Father who has qualified us to be partakers of the inheritance of the saints in the light. He has delivered us from the power of darkness and conveyed us into the Kingdom of the Son of His love."*

Decree 11

(Place your hand upon your heart and pray this prayer.) From this very spot will spring forth a great move and work of God that will impact the whole earth for Christ's Glory!

Cornerstone Scripture

Matthew 28:18-20: *"Jesus came and spoke to them, saying, 'All authority has been given to Me in heaven and on earth. Go therefore and make disciples of all the nations, baptizing them in the name of the Father and of the Son and of the Holy Spirit, teaching them to observe all things that I have commanded you; and lo, I am with you always, even to the end of the age.' Amen."*

Decree 12

Lord, forgive me for wearying You with my sins and iniquities. Thank You, Father, that You do not remember my sins and iniquities. Lord, let us contend together. I put You in remembrance of your promises to forgive and restore me. Father, I state my case. Lord, may we contend together. Lord, that You may acquit me in Your tender mercy and grace.

Cornerstone Scripture

Isaiah 43:26: "*Put Me in remembrance; Let us contend together; State your case, that you may be acquitted.*"

Decree 13

Lord, I confess my sins to You today. Father, I thank You that You see me through the Atoning Blood of Jesus. You forgive me of my sins and You cleanse me and make me righteous in Your sight. I am righteous and I am made holy by the blood of Jesus. I am in right standing with You, Father. I thank You for that today.

Cornerstone Scripture

1 John 1:9: *"If we confess our sins, He is faithful and just to forgive us our sins and to cleanse us from all unrighteousness."*

Decree 14

Lord, I thank You for the Holy Spirit that is within me. Lord, I choose to live a life of prayer today, and I will pray without ceasing. I purpose in my heart to pray in this manner today, and I thank You that You empower me with the precious Holy Spirit to seek You and to pray to You every moment of every day.

Cornerstone Scripture

1 Thessalonians 5:17: *"Pray without ceasing."*

Decree 15

Lord, You formed my heart. Father, I pray that You would re-create in me a clean heart and restore to me a steadfast spirit. Lord, I thank You that you do not cast me away from Your presence. Fill me with Your Holy Spirit anew each day. Fill me now Holy Spirit!

Cornerstone Scripture

Psalm 51:10: *"Create in me a clean heart, O God, And renew a steadfast spirit within me."*

Decree 16

God will never forsake me. Thank You, Father that You are with me always. Your Spirit is within me to guide and teach me continually. I am accepted unconditionally and I will never be rejected by my heavenly Father. Lord, I thank You for Your love and acceptance of me today.

Cornerstone Scripture

Hebrews 13:5: *"I will never leave you nor forsake you."*

Decree 17

Lord, I thank You that You blot out all of my sins and iniquities. Father, You don't remember my sins any longer. My sins are as far as the east is from the west because I am atoned for and restored to right relationship with You by the cleansing blood of Jesus. And today I choose to forgive myself for the times that I have fallen short as well. Amen.

Cornerstone Scriptures

Psalm 103:12: *"As far as the east is from the west, So far has He removed our transgressions from us."*

Isaiah 43:25: *"I, even I, am He who blots out your transgressions for My own sake; And I will not remember your sins."*

Decree 18

Father, I thank You that I am led by Your Spirit, and I thank You that You have given to me the Holy Spirit who guides and teaches me. Lord, I am Your child. I am Your (son/ daughter). So I am led by Your Spirit. Lord, I thank You that the Holy Spirit is going to lead me today.

Cornerstone Scripture

Romans 8:14: *"For as many as are led by the Spirit of God, these are sons of God."*

Decree 19

Lord, I bless You today with all of my soul. I bless Your Holy name, and, Father, I thank You that You forgive all of my sins and heal *All* of my sicknesses. I am forgiven and healed in Jesus' name.

Cornerstone Scripture

Psalm 103:1-3: *"Bless the LORD, O my soul; And all that is within me, bless His holy name! Bless the LORD, O my soul, And forget not all His benefits: Who forgives all your iniquities, Who heals all your diseases."*

Decree 20

Lord, I worship You today, and I thank You for Your angelic host that work on Your behalf. I declare that Your angels heed Your word. Lord, as I confess Your word over my life, Your angels are being released to perform Your word on my behalf. I release and welcome God's angels to bring Your promises into full manifestation in my life and circumstance in Jesus name. Amen!

Cornerstone Scripture

Psalm 103:20: *"Bless the LORD, you His angels, Who excel in strength, who do His word, Heeding the voice of His word."*

Decree 21

Father, I thank You that You are the Good Shepherd. I shall not lack any good thing. You supply all of my needs by Christ Jesus. Lord, I thank You for restoring and healing my soul today, in Jesus name. Amen

Cornerstone Scripture

Psalm 23:1-3: *"The LORD is my shepherd; I shall not want. He makes me to lie down in green pastures; He leads me beside the still waters. He restores my soul; He leads me in the paths of righteousness For His name's sake."*

Decree 22

Father, today I choose to make You my refuge. I choose to trust in You, my Lord. I make a conscious decision to live and dwell in the secret place. I trust You, and I thank You that no evil shall touch me, in Jesus name, for Your angelic host protects me.

Cornerstone Scripture

Psalm 91:1-2, 9-11: *"He who dwells in the secret place of the Most High Shall abide under the shadow of the Almighty. I will say of the LORD, 'He is my refuge and my fortress; My God, in Him I will trust'... Because you have made the LORD, who is my refuge, Even the Most High, your dwelling place, No evil shall befall you, Nor shall any plague come near your dwelling; For He shall give His angels charge over you, To keep you in all your ways."*

Decree 23

Father, I accept that You love me with an everlasting love and that You are drawing me closer to You with the cords of Your supernatural love, grace, and mercy. Your love for me is unshakable. It's unchangeable. You will never forsake me and You are with me to the ends of the earth. Thank You, Lord, that You have an eternal love for me that shall endure forever.

Cornerstone Scripture

Jeremiah 31:3: *"I have loved you with an everlasting love; Therefore with loving kindness I have drawn you."*

Decree 24

Lord, I thank You that Your Kingdom is within me. Lord, You have placed Your very Sprit within me, and I thank You that Your Kingdom will come on earth as it is in Heaven because Your Kingdom is within me now. Lord, I surrender my spirit, soul, and body to Your Kingdom and thank You that I will demonstrate Your Kingdom with the power of the Holy Spirit everywhere I go today. Lord, I invite Your Kingdom to come in my life today in Jesus' name.

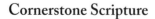

Cornerstone Scripture

Luke 17:21: *"The kingdom of God is within you."*

Decree 25

Oh, Lord, I am asking You to bless me indeed and expand my sphere of influence for Your glory today. Father God, place Your mighty right hand firmly upon me, and protect me. Keep me from evil, and sin. Please do not allow me to cause any harm or pain to my loved ones, neighbors, or myself, in Jesus' name. Amen.

Cornerstone Scripture

1 Chronicles 4:10: *"Oh, that You would bless me indeed, and enlarge my territory, that Your hand would be with me, and that You would keep me from evil, that I may not cause pain!"*

Decree 26

No weapon that is formed against me shall succeed. I condemn every tongue and word curse that has been spoken and that rises up against me. I command every force of darkness associated with these word curses to cease from your assignment. I bind you in the name of Jesus Christ of Nazareth. Lord, I ask You to release Your angels to war on my behalf in the name of Jesus Christ of Nazareth, and bring every negative word spoken against me to naught and to no effect.

Cornerstone Scripture

Isaiah 54:17: *"No weapon formed against you shall prosper, And every tongue which rises against you in judgment You shall condemn. This is the heritage of the servants of the LORD, And their righteousness is from Me," Says the LORD."*

Decree 27

Lord, I just want to bless You with all of my heart and soul! Father, I thank You and I bless You for everything that You have done and everything that You are doing and are going to do as You prosper me, heal me, and transform my life. I choose to take some time and bless You now, for You are very good to me. (Take several minutes to bless the Father, Son, and Holy Ghost for the good things that they have done in Your life today.)

Cornerstone Scripture

Psalm 103:1: *"Bless the LORD, O my soul; And all that is within me, bless His holy name!"*

Decree 28

Lord, I choose to trust in You today, and I will see Your hand move upon my behalf. I shall feed upon Your faithfulness, and You will provide for me. I shall lack no good thing. Lord, I bless You and I thank You for all of the blessings, provisions, and favor that You have given to me. You are my Shepherd and I shall not want. I choose to do good today.

Cornerstone Scripture

Psalm 37:3: *"Trust in the LORD, and do good; Dwell in the land, and feed on His faithfulness."*

Decree 29

Father, I thank You for the ministry of Jesus. Lord, I thank You that after the Lord ascended upon High that the Holy Spirit was given to me. I thank You for the Holy Ghost today. Lord, I thank You that the Holy Spirit is within me and that the precious Holy Spirit will speak to me today. Holy Spirit, I ask You to lead me and guide me in Your preordained paths for me today.

Cornerstone Scriptures

Acts 13:2: "*As they ministered to the Lord and fasted, the Holy Spirit said…*"

Psalm 37:23: "*The steps of a good man are ordered by the LORD, And He delights in his way.*"

Decree 30

Father, Your word teaches me that You will give me Your wisdom in abundance. Lord, I thank You for giving me Your wisdom freely today. Thank You, Lord, that I will walk in the spirit of wisdom and revelation today, and that my steps will be ordered by You today. I am grateful to You, Father, that Your Spirit always guides me to keep me in perfect double peace.

Cornerstone Scripture

James 1:5: *"If any of you lacks wisdom, let him ask of God, who gives to all liberally and without reproach, and it will be given to him."*

Decree 31

Lord, I am healed in the name of Jesus Christ of Nazareth! Father, I thank You that You sent Jesus to take my sins and sickness away on the cross. Lord, I am saved and by the stripes of Jesus I am healed. I will prosper and be in perfect health today even as my soul is saved and prospers.

Cornerstone Scriptures

Matthew 8:17: *"He Himself took our infirmities and bore our sicknesses."*

1 Peter 2:24: *"Jesus bore our sins that we, might live for righteousness—by whose stripes you **were** healed."*

Bonus Word Decree

This shall be a year of extravagant praise! A year of double peace, and supernatural prosperity! Father I thank you that you are releasing your angels to work on my behalf heeding your word, fore you take pleasure to prosper me. Thank you Lord for the great grace, double peace, and supernatural prosperity you are placing upon my life this year. I purpose within my heart to make this a year of extravagant praise as I thank you for your peace and prosperity! Amen

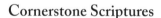

Cornerstone Scriptures

Psalm 148:1-4: "*Praise the LORD! Praise the LORD from the heavens; Praise Him in the heights! Praise Him, all His angels; Praise Him, all His hosts! Praise Him, sun and moon; Praise Him, all you stars of light! 4 Praise Him, you heavens of heavens, And you waters above the heavens!*"

Isaiah 26:3: *"You will keep him in perfect peace, Whose mind is stayed on You, because he trusts in You."*

Psalm 1:3: *"He shall be like a tree Planted by the rivers of water, That brings forth its fruit in its season, Whose leaf also shall not wither; And whatever he does shall prosper."*

Psalm 35:27: *"Let the LORD be magnified, Who has pleasure in the prosperity of His servant."*

Epilogue

In conclusion, I want to encourage you. This short book contains the anointed word of God. God's word is powerful. God's word is sharp, and God's word is able to transform your life and your current situation.

As you are faithful to speak these decrees over your life, you will begin to grow strong in the Lord and the power of His might.

God's word *is* alive, just like Jesus Christ of Nazareth is alive. He *is* risen! And the Messiah loves you with an incredible love that is impossible for us to comprehend with our human minds.

God promised you this amazing guarantee in Isaiah 55:11: "*So shall My word be that goes forth from My mouth; It shall not return to Me void, But it shall accomplish what I please, And it shall prosper in the thing for which I sent it.*"

You see, God's anointed word never fails to accomplish what the Lord has created it to do. God's word will prosper the thing that it is sent out for.

So, as you send out His promises over your life, the word of God will set a supernatural process in motion that will prosper you! I feel a hallelujah fit coming on, and so should you!

So just keep speaking God's word out over your life. Keep confessing His promises out over your circumstances until they begin to change. Keep decreeing these word confessions every day until your life is transformed and revolutionized!

Feed your spirit on the word of God. Feed your spirit just like you nourish your body every day. Remember what the Lord told us, "You shall not live by bread alone, but by every word of God" (see Matthew 4:4; Luke 4:4). Jesus was speaking about feeding your spirit with God's word.

This little book will help you to accomplish that. However, you should read the Bible too. If you are a new believer you should begin by reading the gospels of Matthew, Mark, Luke, and John.

Continue to read these first four books of the New Testament until the words of Jesus are thoroughly absorbed into the very fiber of your spirit and soul.

And remember, it was these same word confessions that transformed my life. And what Jesus did for me He will do for you in a greater measure.

These word confessions helped to take me from poverty to prosperity, from sickness to health, and from the kingdom of darkness to the Messiah's marvelous Kingdom of Light! They will have the same supernatural effect in your life too!

Begin to call those things that do not exist as though they do. And remember to speak these decrees and confessions in the name of Jesus Christ of Nazareth.

The same power that created heaven and earth is endued within that Name. Don't forget that you have been given the right, privilege, and supernatural authority to employ the mighty name of Jesus as you speak and pray and go about your normal day.

And, as you start to speak these decrees, also remember to "But believe". First Corinthians 13:13 tells us this: *"Now abide faith, hope, love, these three; but the greatest of these is love."*

Hope is the emotion that activates faith. In other words, it does not matter how you feel in your mind, you may not "feel" like you have any faith.

However, you can purpose in your heart to have hope, because that is a human emotion. As you confess these decrees, just make up your mind that you will hope that they will work.

Before you know it your hope will grow into faith. Remember that we only need the teeniest little bit of faith for God to begin to remove the mountains in our lives. Remember that faith is really just acting on God's word, faith sprouts from hope.

So expect your hope to mature into faith and expect your faith to mature into love as you see the Lord begin to transform your circumstances as you speak His word over your life!

Don't give up. Remember, it took months before I started getting any breakthroughs, but I just kept right on thanking the Lord for performing His promises that I was speaking over my life.

It took about two and one-half years for the Lord to totally revolutionize my life. And the truth is that He is still on the job today. Jesus is still releasing more favor, more grace, and more blessings into my life every day.

So I just keep on confessing His word, I just keep on thanking God, and as I praise the Lord He keeps on moving mountains out of my way! You will never reach a place where this principle of God's kingdom won't work for you. So just keep on decreeing God's word and reminding God of His promises to you on a daily basis until you pass on into Glory!

Be like the persistent widow (Luke 18:3-5). Just keep on knocking, keep on asking, and keep on stating your case. God is a just and merciful God, and He will give you the justice and everything that is rightfully due to you from His Kingdom.

You can count on it. The Lord is good and His mercy and justice endure forever, and we can expect to see both in our lifetime.

Remember who you are *"in Christ."* You are more than an overcomer in Jesus and you are a joint heir with Christ. You are a child of God and all of the blessings of Abraham are preordained to manifest in your life (Genesis 12; 22; Ephesians 3:8-20).

You are created by God to prosper and be in health even as your soul prospers. You are a royal king and priest. You have the right to go directly before God's throne and state your case.

In fact, that is exactly what you are doing each time that you speak one of these decrees over your life and circumstances. God is listening too, and it won't take long before He will move with power and swiftness on your behalf. He will change your circumstances before you know it.

Finally, don't forget to enforce your boundaries. Keep the breakthrough that you obtain as you decree these scriptural confessions over your life. Learn to live a lifestyle of repentance and forgiveness.

The decrees in this book will help you to ensure that you do just that. Soon you will begin to step into your rightful place as a priest and king.

You will start to sense and know that if God is for you there is no one who can oppose you! God's presence and favor will grow into a reality in your life.

The scriptures tell us this in John 1:5; "*The light shines in the darkness, and the darkness did not comprehend it.*"

Of course, this is speaking about the Messiah, but it is also referring to God's word. As you speak His word out, it is like light that shines into the darkness around your life exorcizing the dark night of your soul.

When you turn on a light switch in your home, it causes the darkness to immediately disappear. Think about decreeing God's word in the same way.

As you speak out the light of God's word over your life using the decrees in this little book, you will be releasing Light into the darkness that has sought to rob you and keep you blind, defeated, and oppressed.

The light of God's word will begin to shine upon that darkness and evil things that have worked to oppress you and keep you in the bondage of the kingdom of darkness.

However, as the Light of God's word shines into the darkness of your life and circumstances, that darkness will not comprehend it. The darkness will disappear, and the enemy of your soul will scamper just like a roach when you turn on the lights!

God is light and in Him is no darkness at all (1 John 1:5). The light of God's word will begin to shine upon your life and you will begin to see a new day dawn, a day of peace and prosperity, a day of grace and favor! Remember the promise found in Job 22: 28: "*You will also declare a thing, And it will be established for you; So light will shine on your ways.*"

When you speak, confess, declare, and prophesy God's word you are releasing heavenly power. You are calling forth abundant life, prosperity, grace, and the favor of the Lord into your circumstances. And the Lord will establish what you confess because you causing His light to shine upon your ways to establish His scriptural promises to manifest in your life.

So decree God's word and let the light of God's scripture shine upon your life! Psalm 119:105 tells us that God's word is a lamp to my feet and a light to my path.

Expect the word of God to shine upon all of your ways and for the Lord of Glory to direct your steps each and every day as His Holy Spirit teaches and guides you.

Expect the same God that created the universe with His words to create a new, prosperous, and blessed life for you as you speak His word over your life and circumstances.

Remember, His word is the same word that created everything. God spoke and said: *"Let there be light,"* and there was! So as you speak that same word over your life, expect the word of God to release light and a new and exciting Divine destiny and life for you! Hallelujah!

So speak this out loud: "I am truly blessed and highly favored, with great great grace, and Divine intervention in my life today. I am a King's kid. I am a royal priest after the order of Melchizedek, and I am walking in the FOG…. the favor of God!" In Jesus name! Amen!

A Prayer of Salvation

The Word of God gives us simple steps to become a new creation and to enter into God's family. You can inherit eternal life and live forever more in paradise or heaven. If you believe in your heart that Jesus Christ of Nazareth was the Son of the living God, and that He died upon the cross to pay for your sins, you can be saved. Romans 10:10 tells you how to be "born again." *"With the heart one believes unto righteousness, and with the mouth confession is made unto salvation."* If you believe this just pray this simple prayer:

Dear heavenly Father, I confess Jesus Christ as Lord. I believe with my heart that Jesus is the Son of God and that He shed His blood and was crucified to pay for my sins. I believe that Jesus did rise from the dead on the third day. I believe that Jesus is alive, and that He will save me now. Lord, I am a sinner. I ask You to forgive my sins and to save me right now. In Jesus' name I pray, Amen.

Lord, I thank You that I am saved! I am a new creature, and I am now in the family of God, I have become the righteousness of God!

If you prayed that prayer, we want to hear from you! Send your name, address, and date you prayed to King of Glory Ministries International, PO Box 903, Moravian Falls, NC 28654, and we will gladly send a free gift to congratulate you on your decision!

Contact The Author

Kevin and Kathy would love to hear your testimonies about how this book has impacted your walk with Christ. To submit testimonies contact them by e-mail.

King of Glory Ministries International is available to teach the material covered in this book in much greater depth. For more information or to order additional resources visit our web page at:

www.kingofgloryministries.org

Email: info@kingofgloryministries.org
Phone: 336-818-1210 or 828-320-3502

Mailing Address:
King of Glory Ministries International
PO Box 903, Moravian Falls, NC 28654

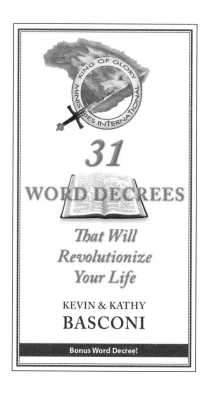

31 WORD DECREES

*That Will
Revolutionize
Your Life*

KEVIN & KATHY
BASCONI

Bonus Word Decree!

To order additional copies of this book please visit
our Resource Center at:

www.kingofgloryministries.org

You can order by phone by calling us Monday
to Friday 10 am-6 pm EST.

Phone: 336-818-1210 or 828-320-3502

Inspirational

King of Glory Ministries International
Pneuma Network

The Breathed Word of God

Watch video teachings with our online video
on demand channel.

Always on.

Always Sharing The Word of God.

Always Free.

Find the Pneuma Network on our homepage.
Just click the black Pneuma Network Icon, or
visit our Media page for free videos, audio Mp3
sermons, or written articles.

www.kingofgloryministries.org

Suggested Reading

Please visit our online resource center for more inspirational books by Kevin Basconi.

Here are some of Kevin's books:
The Sword of the Lord & the Rest of the Lord
Unlocking The Mysteries of the
Seer Anointing
Unlocking The Mysteries of the Powers of the
Age to Come

The Reality Of Angelic Ministry Trilogy
Book 1- *'Dancing With Angels 1, How To Work With The Angels In Your Life'*
Book 2- *'Dancing With Angels 2, The Role Of The Holy Spirit And Open Heavens In Activating Angelic Ministry In Your Life'*
Book 3- *'Dancing With Angels 3, Angels In The Realms Of Heaven'*

Please visit our on-line Resource Center to find more CDs, Mp3's, and other teachings by King of Glory Ministries International

Several Free resources are at this link:
www.kingofgloryministries.org/store/

Moravian Falls
Miniature Art Gallery

Please visit our online art gallery to help support our ongoing humanitarian outreaches to build homes for at risk children and feed widows and orphans at:

www.MoravianFallsminiatureartgallery.com

A portion of the sales of all art purchased from this site will be used to help feed orphans in third world nations. Thanks for your support in this worthwhile cause.

Donate directly to our humanitarian works from Canada, America, or the UK.

You can also donate directly to our orphanage projects and other humanitarian works in the third world. If you are a citizen of Canada, America, or the UK, you can give directly through Hope for the Nations and your gift will be tax deductible in your home nation.

Look for the Hope for the Nations link on the King of Glory Ministries web page:

www.kingofgloryministries.org/donate.php

Partnership

King of Glory Ministries International is reaching out to win the lost and share the love of Jesus around the earth with our soul-winning outreaches every year. We have already seen tens of thousands of people make the decision to pray and receive Jesus Christ as their Lord and Savior.

This is made possible, in part, by generous donations from our friends and ministry partners. Through their help we are ministering the love of the Father to widows and orphans every day, preaching the gospel in publications like this one and in large open air outreach gospel meetings in the third world, with free Mp3 digital sermons and free online teachings and through our new free video on demand internet channel:

The Pneuma Network:
The Breathed Word of God.

To partner with us in these ministries please call us at 336-818-1210 or 828-320-3502 or mail us:

King of Glory Ministries International
P O Box 903, Moravian Falls, NC 28654
or visit our web page at
www.kingofgloryministries.org

Unlocking the Hidden Mysteries of the Seer Anointing

This book contains the teachings the revelations that the Lord has given Kevin over the last 12 year about the seer anointing. We are living in a God ordained moment of time when the seer realm is being released by grace to God's friends (whosoever). This book is designed to help God's people unlock the hidden mysteries of the seer anointing in their lives by understanding the idiosyncrasies of the seer anointing in a Christ centered and sound biblical manner. It is a very through biblical teaching that also is replete with dozens of prayers of activation for the reader (seers).

~~$20.00~~

SALE $15.00

Unlocking the Hidden Mysteries of the Seer Anointing II
The Blessings of Psalm 24

In the new book, *Unlocking the Hidden Mysteries of the Seer Anointing and the Blessings of Psalm 24*, Kevin Basconi continues to open up the hidden mysteries of the seer anointing. This book is a sequel to Kevin's first book on the seer anointing. In it he shares a set of powerful testimonies of angelic visitations and supernatural experiences that were released from the realms of Heaven. On February 25th, 2014 Kevin had a powerful visitation of the spirit of wisdom and revelation and was launched into a seer experience. The Seer Anointing and the Blessings of Psalm 24 is a MUST READ!

Unlocking the Hidden Mysteries
of the Seer Anointing III
The Shaking & The Arising

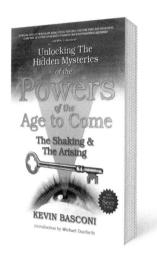

Spiritual gates to heaven are being opened for God's end-time sons and daughters. Kevin Basconi was taken to heaven to teach you how to access these gates!

–SID ROTH, Host, "It's Supernatural!"

~~$20.00~~

SALE $15.00

Activating Your 20/20 Spiritual Vision CD

In this message, *Activating Your 20/20 Spiritual Vision*, Kevin shares several keys that can help you to establish your seer gift and your 20/20 spiritual senses. It is imperative the we become diligent to hear the voice of the Lord and to see what God is doing in our lives at this hour. It is imperative the you develop and build up your ability to discern both good and evil each and every day according to the principle of Hebrews 5:14; Solid food belongs to those who are mature, those who by reason of use have their senses exercised to discern both good and evil. God is seeking to heal and open the spiritual eyes and spiritual ears of His people at this hour. We believe that this message and the prayer of impartation at the end can help spark such a supernatural metamorphosis in your life too!

~~$12.00~~

SALE $9.00

Apostolic Love
CD

This digitally mastered Cd teaching outlines your right and ability to become a royal priest after the order of Melchizedek. The Blood is Jesus Christ and the Apostolic Love of God opens this door to the heavenly realms to each of us.

$12.00

SALE $9.00

Moravian Falls School Of The Seers Box Set 8 CD

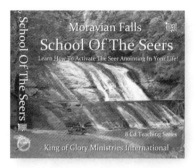

This 8 cd box set is designed to empower you to activate the seer anointing in your life. God created each of us in His image, and as such our spiritual DNA is designed to see and to be seers. We are created to have intimacy and communion with God. We are created to see and hear the Lord clearly. These teaching will help you to activate your ability to hear and see from the realms of heaven clearly. When you activate your seer gifting it can be life changing! This set includes these teachings by Kevin & Kathy Basconi:

Lesson #1 - Disc #1 - What Is The Seer Anointing Lesson #1 - Disc #2 - What Is The Seer Anointing Part #2 Lesson #2 - Disc #3 - Understanding The Seer Anointing Lesson #2 - Disc #4 - Understanding The Seer Anointing Part #2 Lesson #3 - Disc #5 The Seer Anointing & The Gift of Discerning Of Spirits Lesson #4 - Disc #6 The Seer Anointing & Open Heavens Lesson #5 - Disc #7 Activating the Seer Anointing - Part #2 Lesson #5 - Disc #8 Prayers of Impartation To Receive The Seer Anointing - Part #2

~~$85.00~~

SALE $63.75

Entertaining The Heavenly Realms Worship CD

Entertaining the Heavenly Realms featuring Psalmist David Salinas & Friends. This digitally Re-Mastered Cd features over 79 minutes of heavenly soaking and worship music digitally captured at the new International Ministry Apostolic Equipping Center's Worship Room, right from the heart of Moravian Falls, North Carolina.

~~$15.00~~

SALE $12.00

Discerning & Overcoming
The Accuser of the Brethren CD

This 2 Cd message, *Discerning & Overcoming The Accuser of the Brethren*, can transform your life through the anointed Word of God! The anointing breaks the heavy yokes and burdens of darkness and deception. You can learn to set yourself free from yokes of darkness and oppression and as you do your life will be transformed! You can go from hopelessness to hope, from sickness to health, from poverty to prosperity.

~~$12.00~~

SALE $9.00